# American Contemporary
## MASTERS
### A COLLECTION OF WORKS FOR PIANO

ISBN 0-7935-5098-X

## G. SCHIRMER, *Inc.*

DISTRIBUTED BY

HAL•LEONARD
CORPORATION
7777 W. BLUEMOUND RD. P.O. BOX 13819 MILWAUKEE, WI 53213

This collection of late Twentieth-Century works is a remarkable sampling of the diverse music that composers are writing for the piano. Whether casually perused or intensely studied, this volume offers a sampling of the works of some of our finest living American composers. Concert programs, general repertoire, and teaching can be freshened and enlivened by the study and performance of these compositions. By becoming better acquainted with the music in this book, one may be stimulated to investigate other compositions of these vital composers—both for piano and other musical ensembles—and eagerly anticipate the next premiere, performance, and publication of your favorites among them.

# CONTENTS

## PERFORMANCE NOTES

The sound throughout should be soft and resonant. Dynamic levels should never exceed mezzo forte. Special attention should be given to equalizing the volume of both hands so that no line is ever louder than another. In this way the intertwining of patterns can be most successfully realized.

In passages where the proximity of lines is particularly close a quick attack must be used to enable repeated soundings of the notes.

Pedal should be held throughout each passage until the next gate (change of mode) occurs.

San Francisco, December 1977

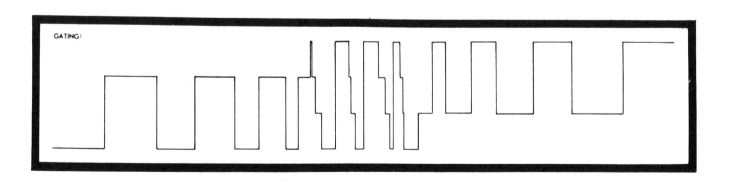

*for Sarah*

# CHINA GATES

John Adams

♩ = 72

4

6

(sempre Ped.)

*(sempre Ped.)*

*pp*

*(hold pedal throughout)*

9

*(hold pedal throughout)*

*morendo al fine*

*dedicated to Charles Ives*

# THEY ALL SANG YANKEE DOODLE

Dave Brubeck
Edited by Thomas Pierson

Flowing, not too slow

Slowly (in 2)

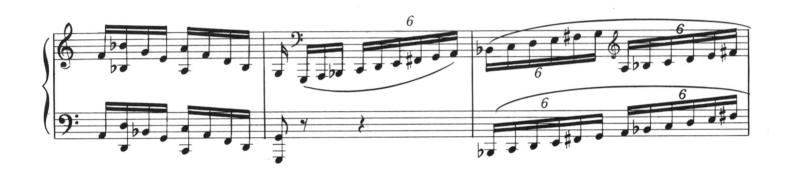

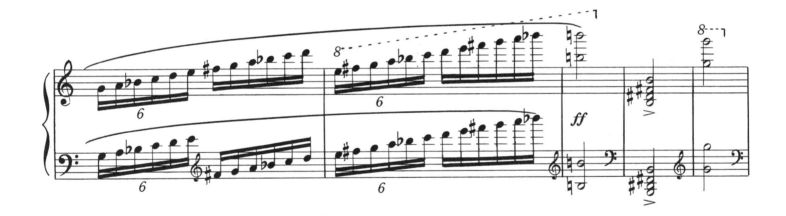

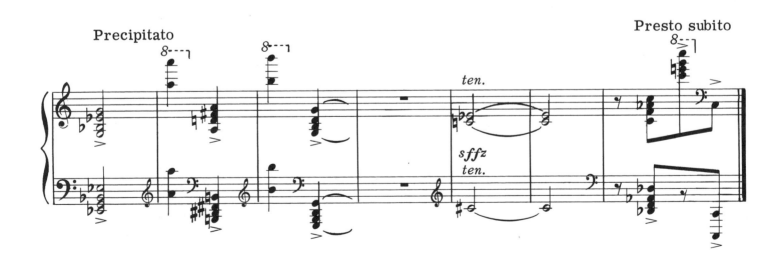

*for Sheldon Shkolnik*
# ADAGIO
from *Gazebo Dances*

John Corigliano
arranged by Dolores Fredrickson

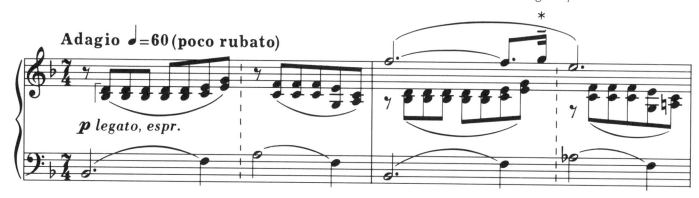

\* Always make a slight *ritard.* on the sixteenth note and return to tempo on the next beat.

38

*to Christopher O'Riley*

# MARDI GRAS

from *The Enchanted Garden*

Richard Danielpour
(1992)

**Wild and uninhibited** ♩ = 120 – 126

Lo stesso tempo, ma più tranquillo

(Ped. as needed)

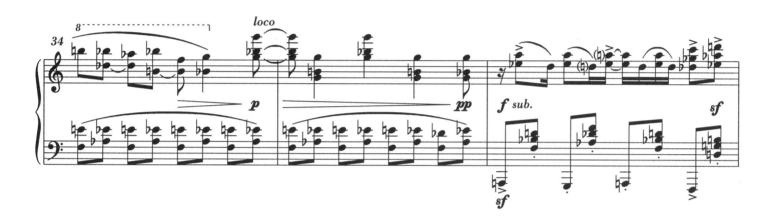

**Ben misurato (lo stesso tempo)** ♩ = 120 – 126

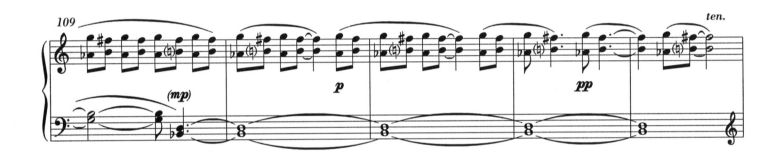

**Lo stesso tempo**

(Ped. as needed)

# MIDDLE PASSAGE

Anthony Davis
(1983)

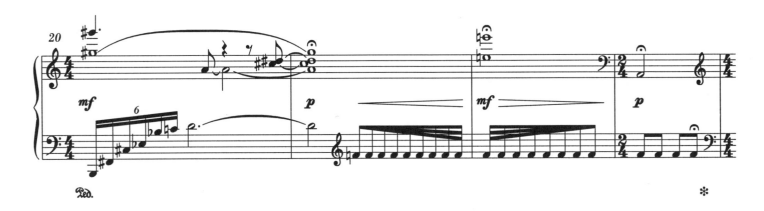

Improvise (jagged, contrasting rhythms)

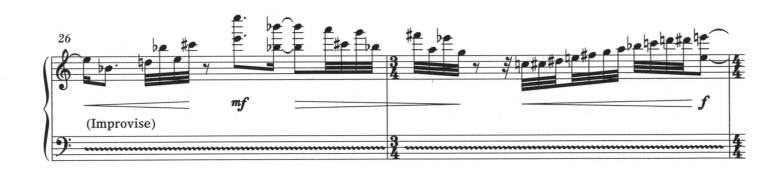

(Improvise)

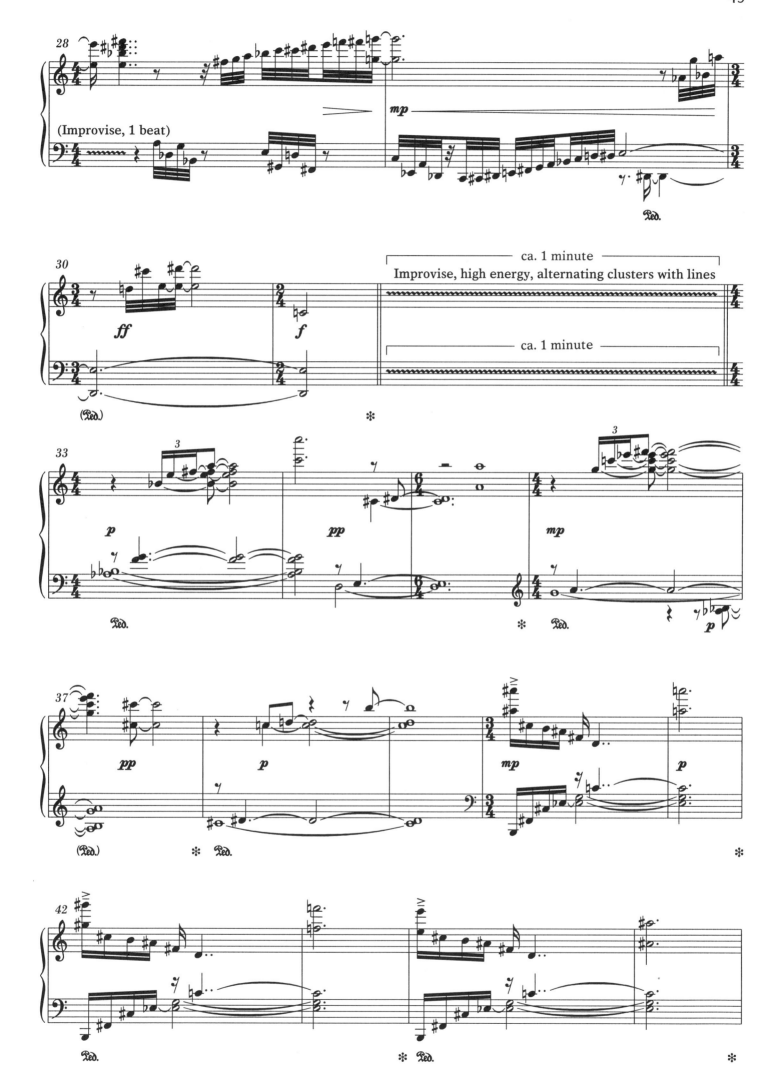

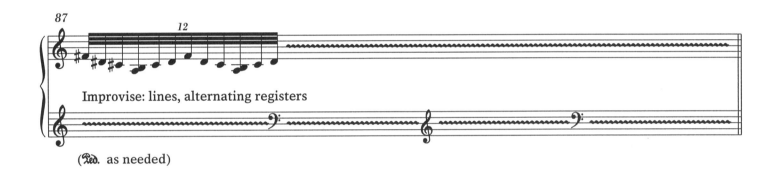

Improvise: lines, alternating registers

(Ped. as needed)

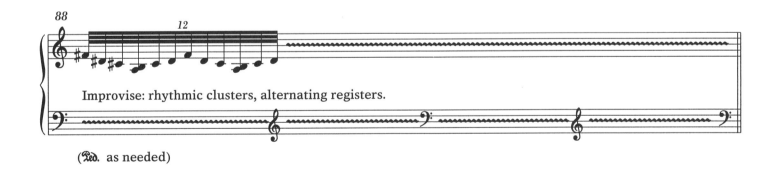

Improvise: rhythmic clusters, alternating registers.

(Ped. as needed)

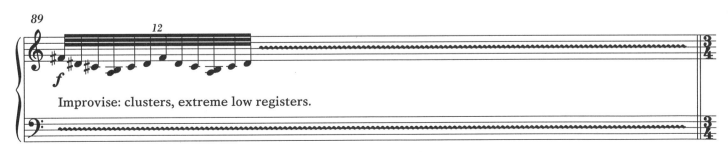

Improvise: clusters, extreme low registers.

(Ped. as needed)

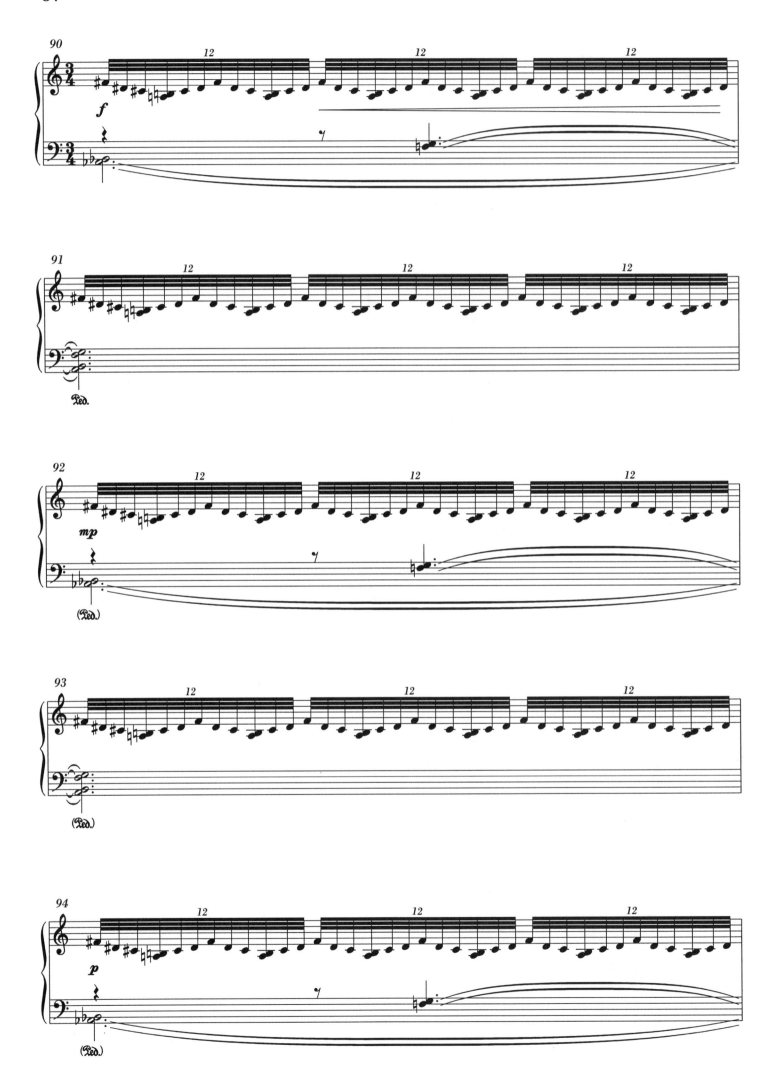

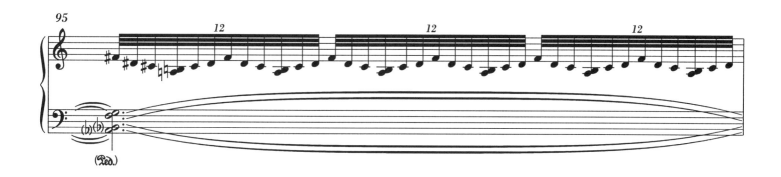

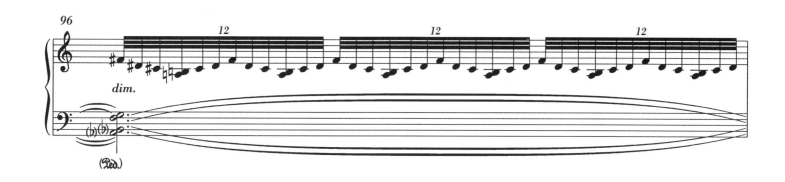

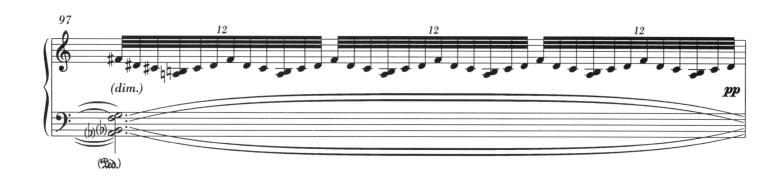

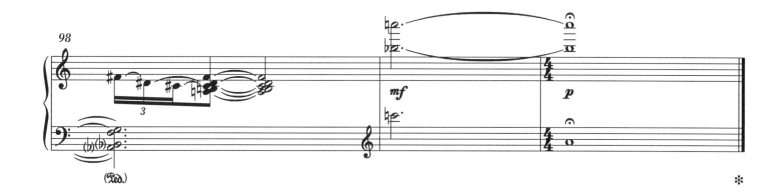

# SALUTE TO SCARLATTI
## A Suite of Sonatas
for Piano or Harpsichord

Norman Dello Joio

# I

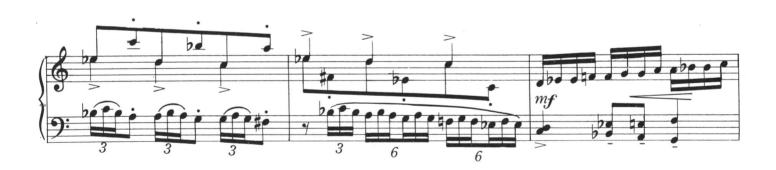

# II

62

# III

Allegro moderato e grazioso ♩ = 76

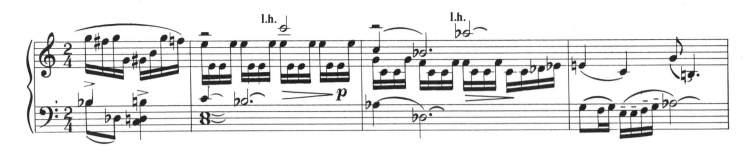

# IV

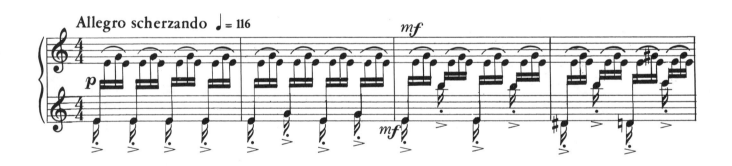

accelerando a tempo primo

# WICHITA VORTEX SUTRA

Philip Glass

74

121 **Flowing** ( ♩ = 120 )

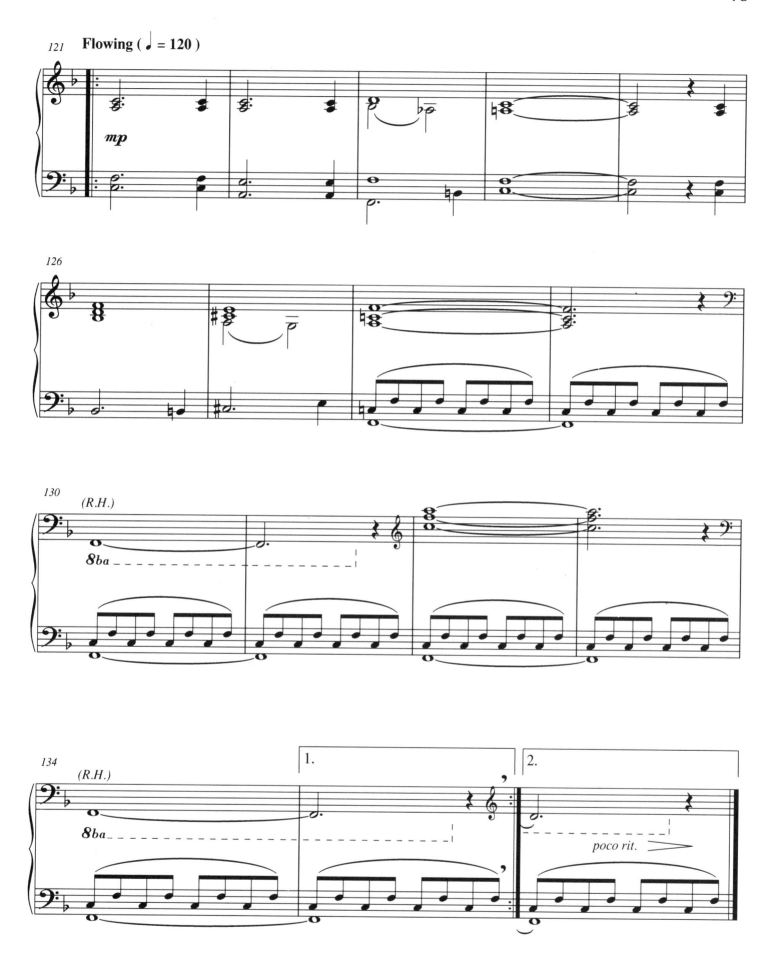

# CHINA CHIPS

from *Pieces of China*

Morton Gould

78

80

2'45"

*Commissioned by the U.S. Information Agency for the Artistic Ambassador Program*

# PATTERNS
## 1

Morton Gould

*Commissioned by the U.S. Information Agency for the Artistic Ambassador Program*

# PATTERNS
## 7

Morton Gould

*for John Boros*

# GOSPEL SHOUT
from *Four Occasional Pieces*

John Harbison
(1978)

*for André Previn's birthday*

# TWO PART INVENTION

from *Four Occasional Pieces*

John Harbison
(1983)

**Con moto, rubato**

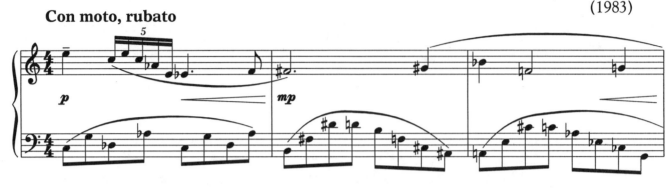

*for Joan Tower*

# MINUET
from *Four More Occasional Pieces*

John Harbison
(1987)

*for Rosie Harbison*

# ANNIVERSARY WALTZ

from *Four More Occasional Pieces*

John Harbison
(1987)

col Ped.

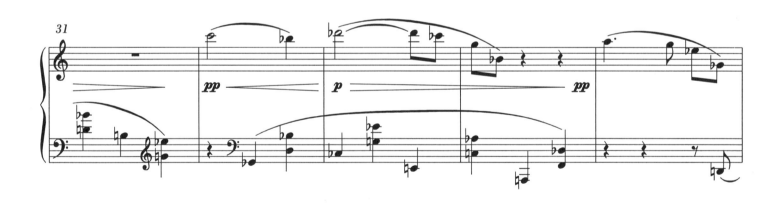

*to Stanley Babin*

# NARRATIVE

Lee Hoiby

to Lauri
# LULLABY
from *Before Sleep and Dreams*

Aaron Jay Kernis
(1987)

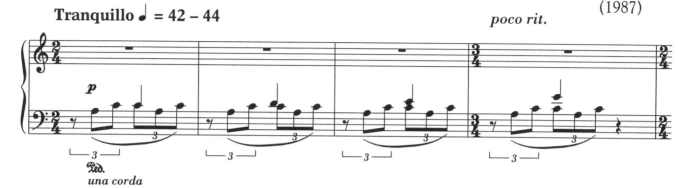

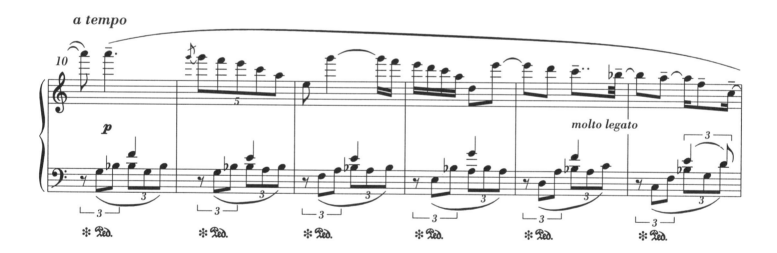

*appassionato*

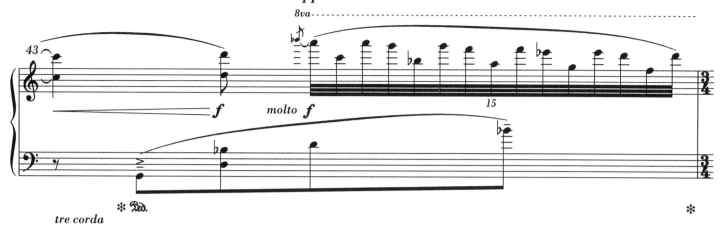

tre corda

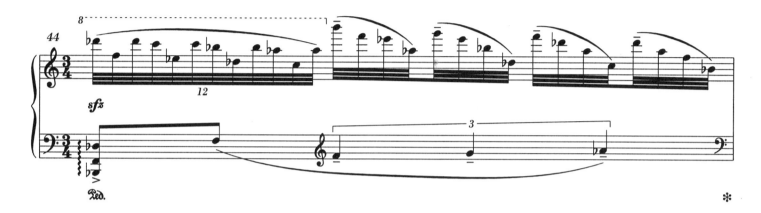

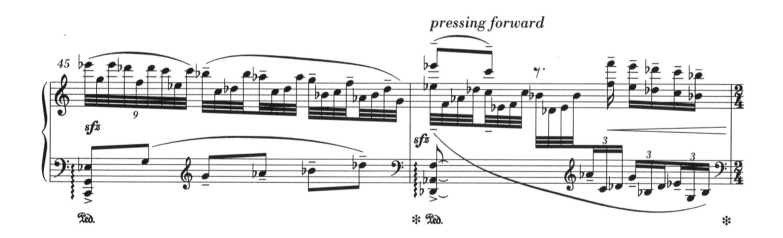

*pressing forward*

*allarg. molto*  **Tempo I** ($\bullet$ = 42 – 44)

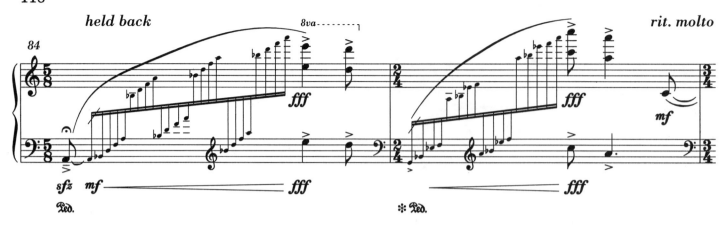

**Tempo I, tranquillo**

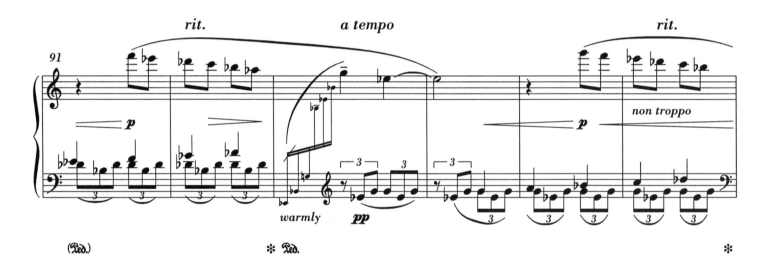

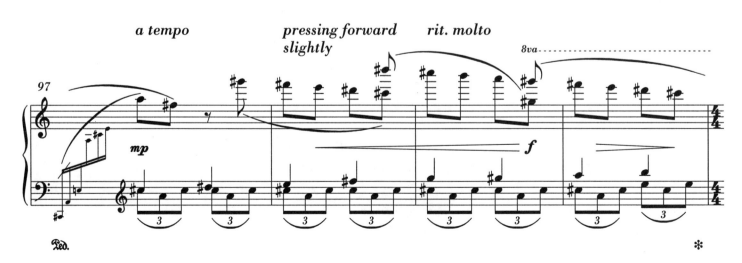

# FIVE PIECES FOR PIANO

(to be played in one movement)

**1.**

Leon Kirchner

2.

(continue)

*Only E♮ sounds.

## 3.

126

4.

# 5.

*to Peter Serkin*

# BREEZE OF DELIGHT

from *Fantasy Pieces*

Peter Lieberson
(1989)

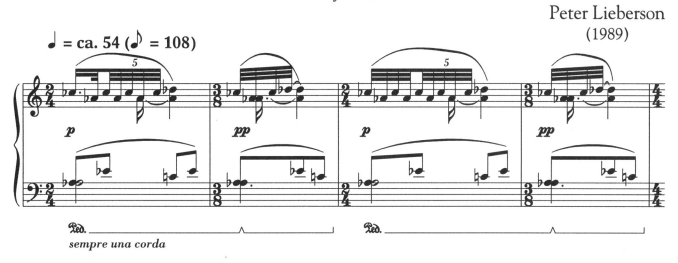

*sempre una corda*

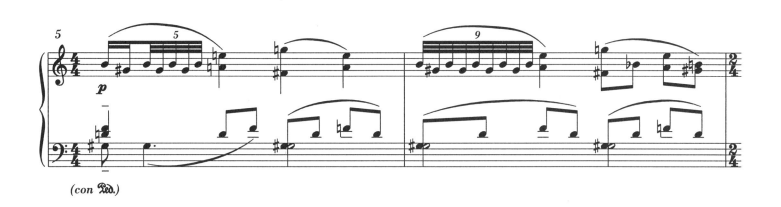

*(con Ped.)*

*allarg.*     *a tempo*

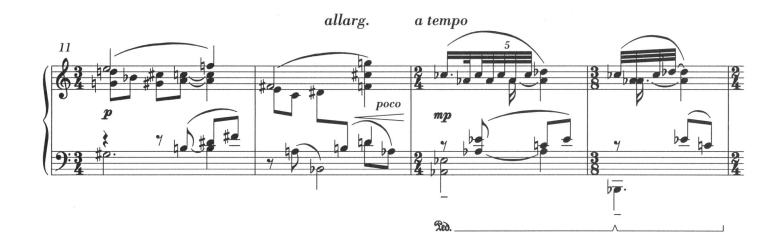

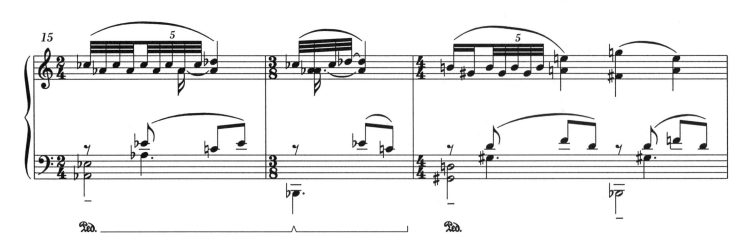

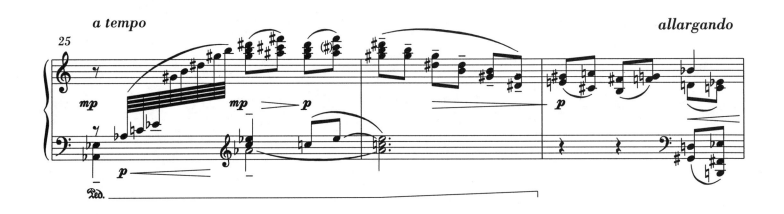

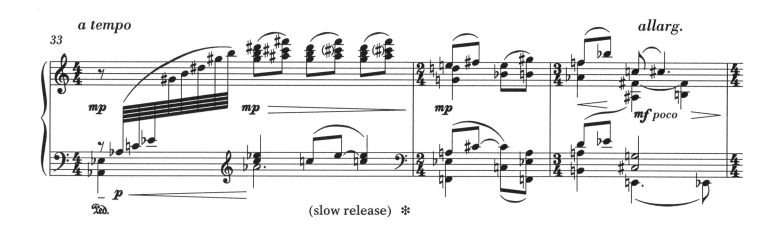

# MEMORY'S LUMINOUS WIND
from *Fantasy Pieces*

Peter Lieberson
(1989)

Chorale
*(Jonathan Lieberson and James Kearney, in memoriam)*

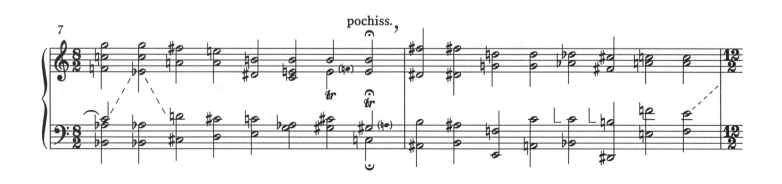

*attacca*

Motet
*(Goddard Lieberson in memoriam)*

**Stesso Tempo** ♩ = 72

# PRELUDE

Mel Powell

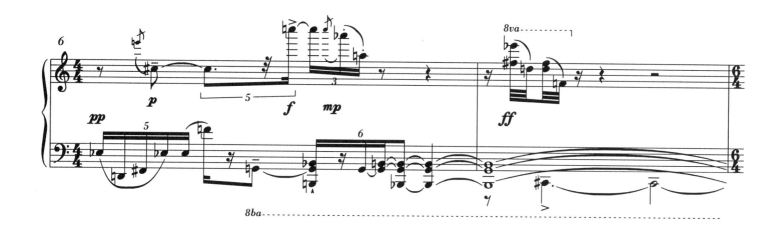

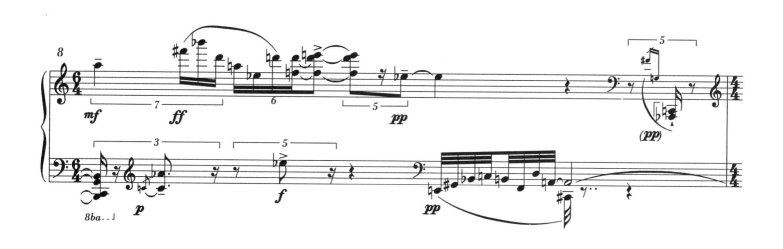

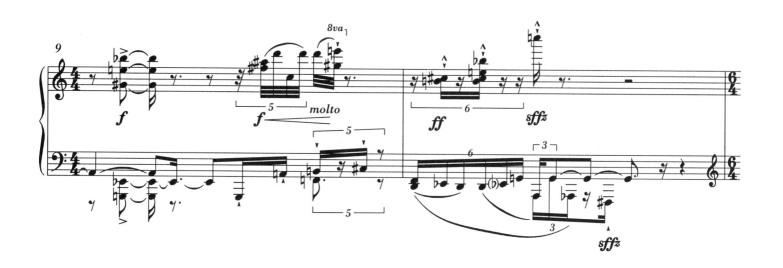

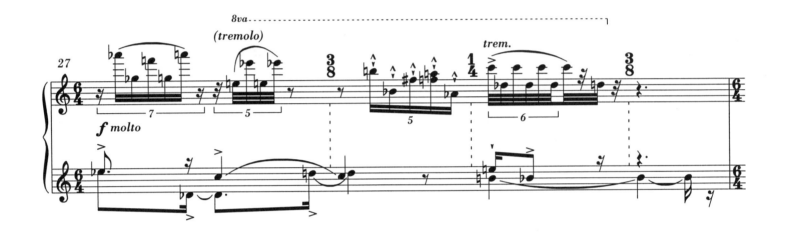

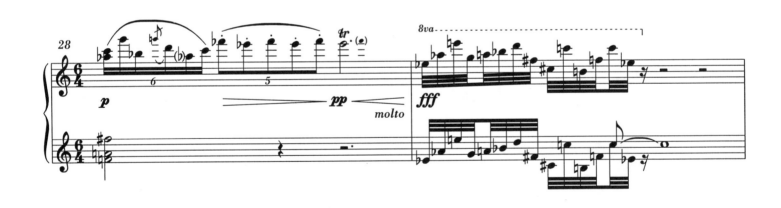

*for Ursula*

# "OR LIKE A... AN ENGINE"

Joan Tower
(1994)

non Ped.

\* Note: throughout the piece, the sixteenth note remains constant, unless a 'tuplet is indicated.

**A tempo** (♩ = ca. 132)

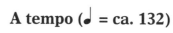

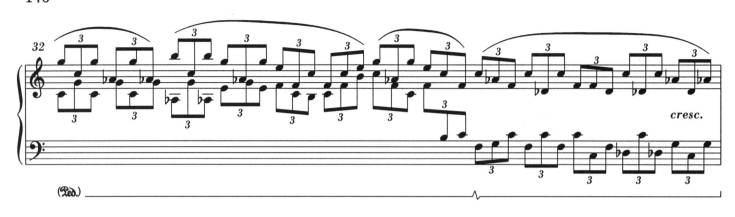

**Poco meno mosso** ($\quarternote$ = ca. 120)

*poco rit.*

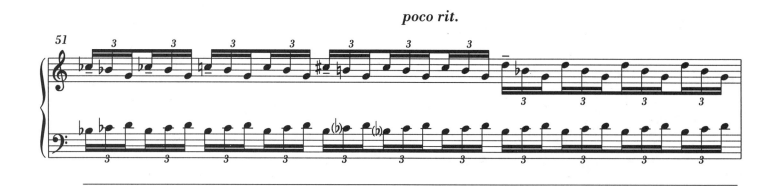

**A tempo** ($\quarternote$ = ca. 132)

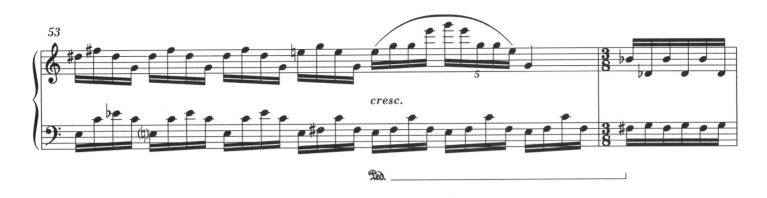

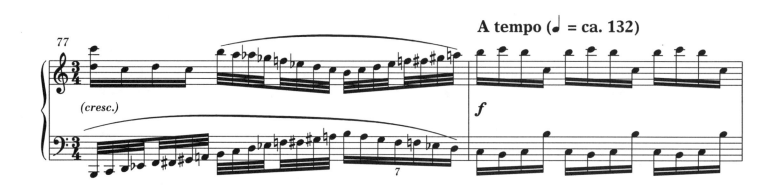

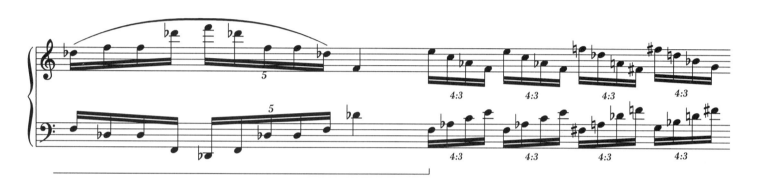